A Coloring Book
by Shannon Houchin

Copyright © 2023 by Shannon Houchin

All rights reserved. No part of this publication may be reproduced, distributed, or transmitted in any form or by any means, including photocopying, recording, or other electronic or mechanical methods, without the prior written permission of the publisher, except in the case of brief quotations embodied in critical reviews and certain other noncommercial uses permitted by copyright law. For permission requests, write to the author: shannon@shannonhouchin.com

TEXAS FRUIT

FARM STAND

PEACH ORCHARD

PEACH

WATERMELON PATCH

BLACK DIAMOND WATERMELON

BLUEBERRIES

RUBY RED GRAPEFRUIT

CANTALOUPE

PECOS CANTALOUPE

ORANGE ORCHARD

TX NAVAL ORANGE

EAST TX TOMATOES

FIGS

FINN AND STUBBS

TEXAS VEGETABLES

FARM STAND

OKRA

BICOLOR SWEET CORN

GREEN BEANS

ZUCCHINI

CABBAGE

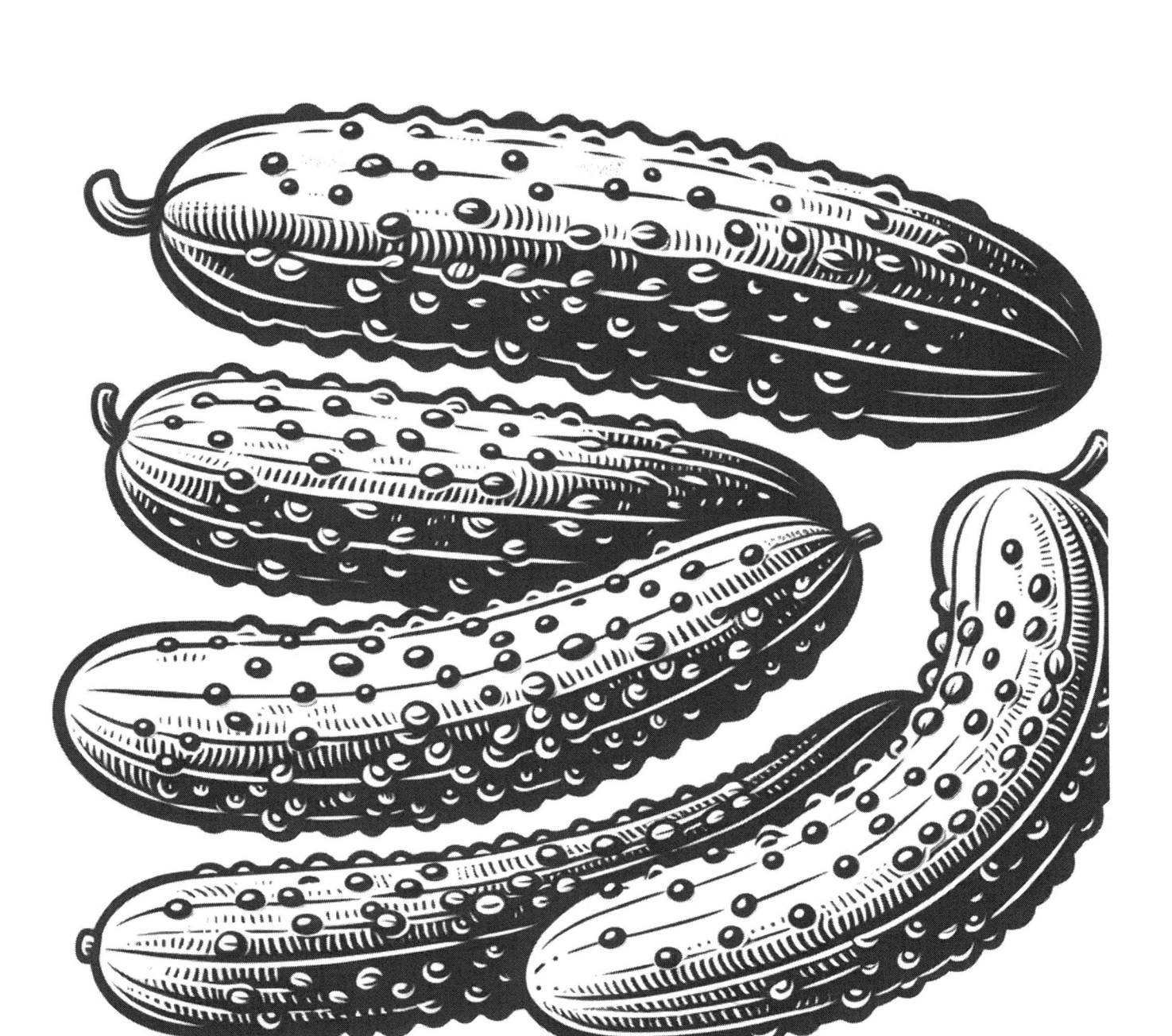

RED RIVER PICKLES

SPINACH

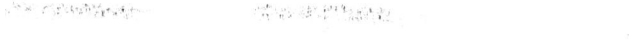

CARROTS

SWEET POTATOES

BLUEBONNETS

OTHER STUFF WE LOVE IN TEXAS

TEXAS PECANS!

HONEY

TEXAS

Made in the USA
Columbia, SC
15 August 2024